Mo's Photo

Written by Amanda Cant

Illustrated by Julie Park

Rosie and Mo saw a man.

He had a camera and some lights.

Mrs Hall said, 'Stop, everybody. Put your books down.'

Rosie sat down. She looked at the camera and smiled.

Then Bobby sat down. He looked at the camera and smiled.

Then Mo sat down. She looked at the camera. But she didn't smile.

She looked down . . . and

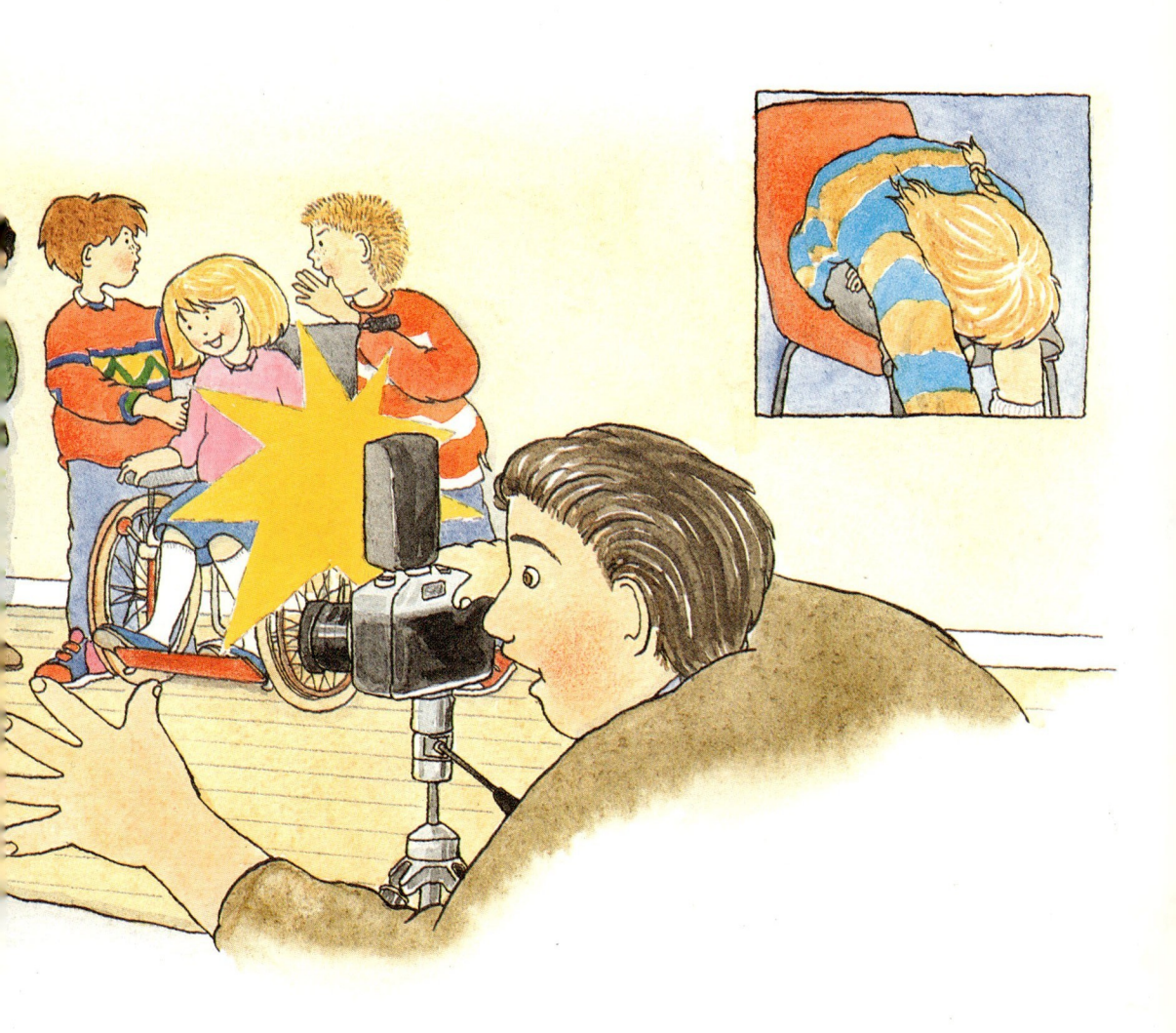

the camera flashed.

Mo looked round . . . and

the camera flashed.

Mo sneezed . . . and

the camera flashed.
Mrs Hall was cross.

Then Mrs Hall sneezed.
Everybody laughed.

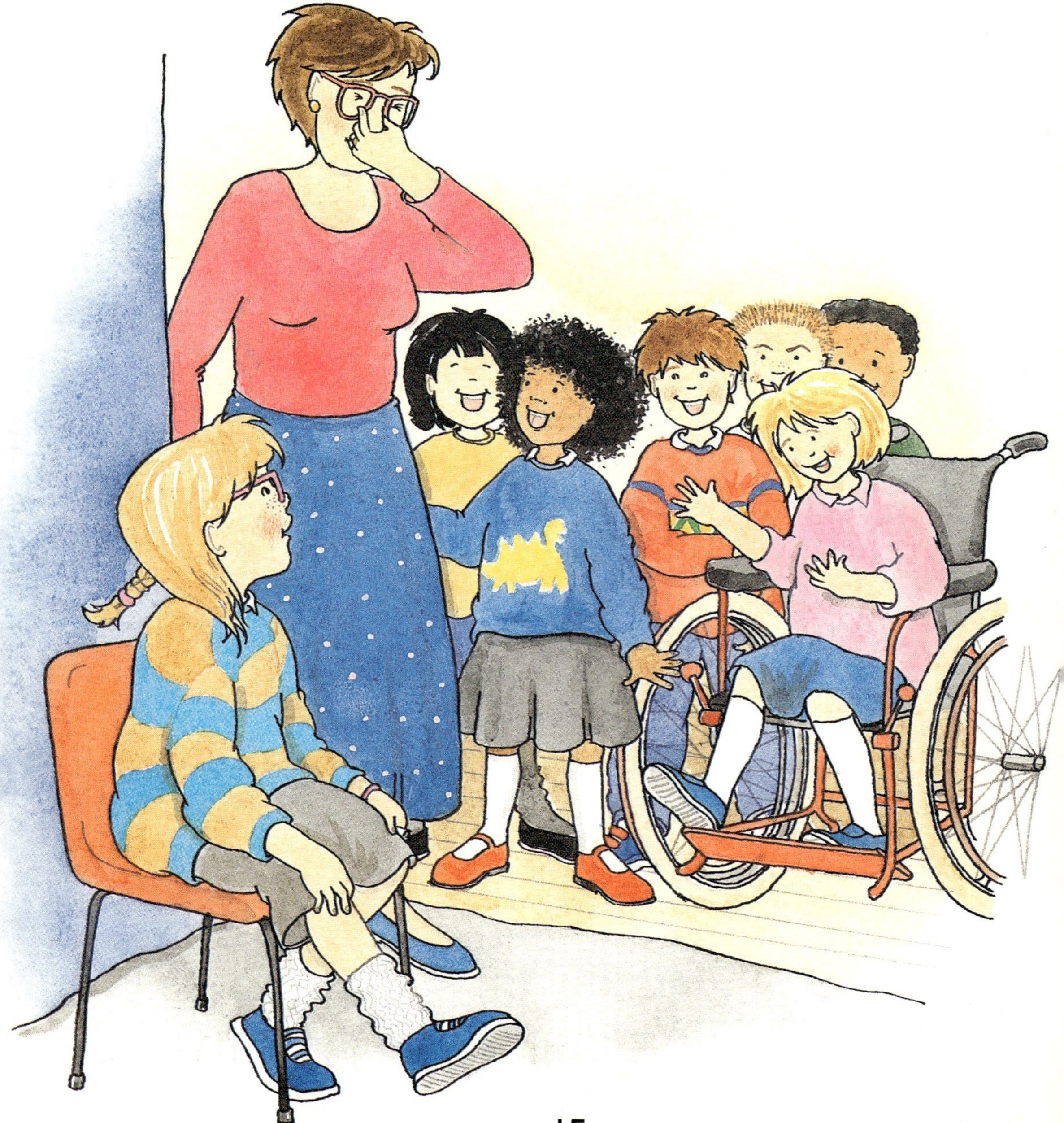

And so did Mo.